A GUIDE TO TUITION-FREE EDUCATION ABROAD

ALSO, BY **COLLINS O. ELESIRO**

The Triumvirate of Life
(Earth, Humankind, and Volition)

A GUIDE TO
TUITION-FREE
EDUCATION ABROAD

HOW TO STUDY ABROAD FOR FREE

COLLINS OBINNA ELESIRO

Crystalinks

EDUCATION

For permission requests, write to the publisher, addressed "Attention: Permissions Coordinator," at the address below.

CRYSTALINKS EDUCATION INTERNATIONAL

(A part of Crystalinks Investment and Services Ltd)

www.crystalinkseducation.com

Info@crystalinkseducation.com

First Printing: October 2016

First Revised Edition September 2019

ISBN: 978-1-326-73736-8

DEDICATION

The entire content of this book is dedicated to my dear step-mother, Mrs. Joy Ulumma Elesiro for her immeasurable support and encouragement, and to You who realises the importance of knowledge.

Collins Elesiro

"KNOWLEDGE IS POWER. INFORMATION IS LIBERATING. EDUCATION IS THE PREM-ISE OF PROGRESS, IN EVERY SOCIETY, IN EVERY FAMILY".

- KOFI ANNAN

CONTENTS

ACKNOWLEDGEMENT

At times like this, it is only natural to acknowledge and appreciate the immeasurable and unrelenting efforts of people who have directly or indirectly contributed to the successful completion of this book.

First and foremost, my unalloyed and profound gratitude goes to Almighty God whose divine providence has enabled the successful completion of this book.

My special thanks also go to Professor Dr B. R. Duncan for his encouragement and support, and for editing this book and writing the Foreword.

I owe a deep and unreserved gratitude to my research team of dedicated content writers; Mr. Gideon Chukwuemeka, Mr. Chimezie Anerobi, and Mr. Alex Kadiri for their immense contribution towards the completion of this book.

FOREWORD

Academic education is crucial to some aspects of white-collar career advancement. Tertiary education bodies compete in a highly competitive market to recruit students. Furthermore, the fees – especially from international students add to the GDP of countries. However, on the other side of the coin are struggling parents who do not have the finance available to support their children's higher education needs. Many adults, also keen to fine-hone their degrees, cannot find a pot of gold to support their desire to move up the academic ladder and this advance their career.

Debates continue to swirl down corridors, and arguments about rights, privilege and entitlement muddy the post-school educational waters. However, Collins Elesiro has avoided self-defeating discussions and opened the doors of opportunity for those who are prepared to walk the extra mile that could end in the discovery of accredited educational bodies offering FREE education.

While reading through the well-researched information, readers will be enabled to pursue avenues that could end the futile efforts of many sincere and aspiring students to find educational opportunities. While there is no pot of gold at the end of the rainbow of promise, Collins has nevertheless shown us where we can knock on doors that could provide that one chance in a lifetime – free education.

We are indebted to the author for his research, and I am

sure that many will have cause to thank him because, after following the pathways outlined in this publication, their search for academic education could morph from a dream into reality!

Thank you, Collins.

Professor Dr B. R. Duncan

April 2019

PREFACE

During my many years as an Education Consultant, I have heard people lament the need for insightful information that not just feeds them snippets but also gives them a complete step by step rundown of the process involved in applying for international education. For example, different clients needed to know which universities offer scholarships while others wanted free education programme. Due to the dearth of information, many students wishing to benefit from international education had to choose the more easily understood local opportunities.

However, all is not lost! In 1975, Eppie Lederer said, "If you think education is expensive – try ignorance". Her axiomatic comment was a reaction to parental concerns about tax deductibility possibilities for her children's' education. Now, some four decades later, I am still inundated with enquiries about free education and scholarships abroad – Lederer's insightful words remain true. Currently, many students cannot have the quality and affordable education they desire and deserve, not because it is expensive per se, but because of an ignorance of the fact that they can have quality, tuition-free education abroad. However, why have they not had the opportunity to discover the facts?

In my quest to provide answers in this information-packed guide, I have researched information about different universities across the globe and listed information about reputable international institutions that merit attention. This publication provides students and sponsors with valuable information about countries and institutions that offer tuition-free studies. The content contains the "where" and "how" of a no fees education abroad.

Consequently, this book focuses on three educational needs (the 3-Es):

1. Exposition: readers will discover information about countries, institutions, and the requirements for tertiary education that includes contact details: phone numbers, website, and email information that opens avenues for further enquiries and information. Readers will journey across Asia to Europe; from America to Australia. Get on board!

2. Education: readers will learn about tuition-free studies and enter the fascinating world of striking cultures. For example, did you know that Austria is the home of the iconic musical Sound of Music, and home to the world-renowned actor-cum-politician, Arnold Schwarzenegger? Ah, but there is more to learn, is there not.

3. Enlightenment: A tuition-free education is not a fairy tale; it is not a hoax. Furthermore, an international student will also gain first-hand knowledge and experience of different and exciting social and cultural realities – we all live in one global village.

Collins Obinna Elesiro

October 2016

INTRODUCTION

Little is known about tuition-free colleges and universities globally. For some, reality only happens in films!

So, to bring reality within the grasp of readers, this book is a step by step guide on how to gain admission to tuition-free universities in the United States, the United Kingdom, Sweden, Germany, Austria, Australia, Norway, Finland, Denmark, Japan, the United Arab Emirates, and South Africa. Furthermore, there are fantastic scholarship opportunities for underprivileged individuals from developing countries – for FREE! There are other online university courses for those who wish to gain a fully recognised international education certificate from the comfort of their homes – travel-free!

Interestingly, EU/EEA Nationals, are entitled to free tuition fee in most countries in Europe. However, the UK's tuition fees apply to both Home, EU/EEA nationals and international students alike. Nonetheless, Home students and EU/EEA Nationals in the UK can apply for a student loan that covers all tuition fee for the duration of their course. Do not forget that the loan must be repaid after graduation when the student finds employment with a minimum annual income of £17,495.

Consequently, UK Nationals not wishing to carry student debt after graduation might decide to study at a tuition-free university in other parts of Europe and, as a bonus, make use of their free time to explore different scenery, and become acquainted with different cultures – a unique international exposure that could also boost a CV! However, if the UK leaves the EU, this option might not apply – so, check with the appropriate government website.

Despite all efforts put in place to maintain the accuracy of the information in this book, it is possible that one or more of the scholarships or tuition-free institutions listed have been changed in some way or even discontinued. To avoid disappointment or misunderstandings, verify all information with the appropriate college or university.

Also, please be aware that there might be other institutions that offer grants, financial aid, and awards other than those listed in this book.

CHAPTER 1: UNITED STATES OF AMERICA

Why study in USA?

The United States is a massive country with a considerable population, land mass, and diverse ethnic groups. Alongside, are interesting historical sites and modern places of interest. Applying to colleges, universities and for scholarships can take time, but the rewards of an American degree will impact on a student's life and outweigh any time lags.

Also, the United States offers work-study opportunities to international students such as working during the day and taking evening or weekend classes, part-time and even with fulltime employment, working on- and off-campus, and receiving American dollars!

Berea College

According to www.berea.edu, "Berea College is the only school in the United States that provides 100% funding to 100% of enrolled American and international students".

- College Location: Berea, KY
- Speciality: Liberal arts college. The student is awarded a 4-year, tuition scholarship work-study programme

In many cases, the college can offer additional financial aid to assist with a room, board, and other expenses, not loans, according to need. Simply put, students at Berea College pay what they can afford. The advantage is in the nationally recognised academic and extracurricular activities. The college offers on-campus employment and a laptop computer as part of the 4-year tuition scholarship.

Berea's Tuition Promise Scholarship

This scholarship is combined with the financial aid possible as well as any other scholarship you may be awarded by outside parties or organisations to cover 100% of tuition costs. For most Berea students, the Tuition Promise Scholarship amounts to nearly $100,000 over four years.

So, when you enrol at Berea, your scholarship will be provided by people you don't even know but who believe in your potential - Berea is well-positioned to help you realise your potential.

What are the admissions requirements?

- Applicants must meet university entrance requirements in their own country and be able to present outstanding secondary or leaving exam results
- Applicants must submit a complete application packet, that must arrive at the Office of Admissions before the deadline – 30 November of the enrolment year
- Applicants must also present results from one of the following approved standardised tests: TOEFL, IELTS, ACT or SAT I. Applicants must submit scores from only one of these four tests

Contact

Office of Admissions CPO 2220

Berea, KY 40404

Phone: 859-985-3000

Toll-Free: 800-326-5948

Fax: 859-985-3512

Office Hours

Monday -Friday, 8:00 a.m.-5:00 p.m. Saturday,
By Appointment. Sunday, Closed.

For more information, visit www.berea.edu.

The Fulbright Foreign Students Programme

The Fulbright Programme is a scholarship programme supportive of international students studying for a Master's or PhD degree. The grant will cover the tuition fee, textbooks, airfare, living stipend, and health insurance as agreed with the host institutions.

Courses for both Masters and PhD degrees, including interdisciplinary studies are covered under this programme - except for a medical or research degree.

The deadline for applications depends on the country of the applicant. An example is the Nigerian Fulbright applications that commence in February and end in May.

Prospective foreign applicants can visit the programme website for more information about the scholarship. Non-U.S. citizens must contact the Fulbright Commissions/Foundation or the U.S. Embassy in their home country for information and application forms. However, If an applicant's home country is not listed on the site, information is available at www.fundingusstudy.org to review study abroad programmes operating in their home country. Web: http://foreign.fulbrightonline.org/

United States Scholarship to Africa

This programme offers assistance to citizens of African descent at the undergraduate and postgraduate levels, to attain their education and qualifications from universities and colleges in the United States.

Recipient's Qualifications

Africans over the age of 18 are eligible to apply for the scholarship and must meet the basic requirements as stated on the scholarship site. The selection of candidates begins when the first 5,500 entries are received and verified. Successful candidates are notified by the end of the first quarter of the following year.

Recipient's Entitlement

Free tuition and an additional annual allowance of US$3,000 is provided for welfare; assistance in securing a study time-limited Student Visa that will expire at the end of the programme.

Recipients can also engage in part-time jobs to earn extra income.

Please visit the scholarship website for more information. http://www.ussafrica.org.

Email: helpdesk@ussafrica.org
Fax: +1-360-3631468

Mastercard Foundation
Scholars Programme

The MasterCard Foundation Scholars programme seeks to educate and develop bright and economically marginalised young people from Africa and developing countries who show a willingness to contribute to the transformation of their countries.

The programme aims to help transition promising young people from beneficiaries to benefactors, preparing them with the values, knowledge, skills, and leadership required to fuel economic and social progress across the world.

The scholarship will provide necessary financial support and provide an avenue for mentorship programmes to develop critical reasoning and entrepreneurship.

The following US universities are partnering with MasterCard Foundation to offer these scholarships for students from Africa and developing countries.

Mastercard Foundation Scholars Programme at Wellesley College

Wellesley College provides nine (9) African women with scholarships, mentoring, counselling, and internship opportunities for undergraduate studies. The students will arrive in groups of three students each year.

For application procedures and suitable decision plans and deadlines, visit www.wellesley.edu/admission.

Mastercard Foundation Scholars Programme at Arizona State University (ASU)

Arizona State University takes in ten (10) undergraduate students from Africa to educate and give them the knowledge to develop their countries. It will support 270 Mastercard Foundation Scholars over 10 years (2012-2022).

Level of Study: undergraduate degree

Application deadline is usually:

Admission application: 01 January

Scholarship deadline: February 01

Mastercard Foundation Scholars Programme at the University of California, Berkeley

At the University of California Berkeley, the scholars will pursue both undergraduate and professional master's degrees.

Level of Study: Undergraduate and Master's Degree

Application Deadline usually falls during:

For Undergraduate: 30th November and for the Master's between   1st December and 8th January.

Mastercard Foundation Scholars Programme at the Michigan State University (MSU)

The MasterCard Foundation has partnered with Michigan State University to provide full tuition scholarships to undergraduate and graduate students from Sub-Saharan Africa.

The university will receive $45 million in funding from the foundation to support 185 scholars throughout the nine-year programme, which includes 100 four-year undergraduates and 85 Master's degree students.

Mastercard Foundation Scholars Programme at Duke University

Full tuition and living stipends are provided to MasterCard Scholars at Duke University. Annually, a total of thirty-five (35) Scholars are accepted in batches of seven (7).

Level of Study: Undergraduate Degree
Previous Application Deadline: January

Other Institutions in partnership with the MasterCard Foundation Scholars Programme are:

- African Leadership Academy
- African Institute for Mathematical Sciences
- American University of Beirut – Faculty of Health Sciences
- Ashesi University

- BRAC
- Camfed
- EARTH University
- Equity Group Foundation Wings to Fly
- FAWE
- KNUST
- Makerere University
- McGill University
- The University of Edinburgh
- University of British Columbia
- University of Cape Town
- University of Pretoria
- University of Toronto

For more information on the MasterCard scholars programme, visit the MasterCard Foundation website. http://www.mastercardfdn.org/scholars-programme/

Hubert H. Humphrey Fellowships for International Students

The Humphrey programme was initiated in 1978 to honour the memory and accomplishments of the late Senator and Vice-President of the United States, Hubert H. Humphrey and is for mid-level professionals.

The programme is designed to meet the requirements of policy makers, planners, administrators, and managers in the government, public and private sectors, and non-governmental organisations, who have a public service commitment, demonstrated leadership potential, and commitment to their own country's development. Women and candidates from minority and disadvantaged groups are encouraged to apply.

Candidates should be proficient in both written and spoken English and will be required to take the Internet-based Test (IBT) of English as a Foreign Language (TOEFL).

Host institutions include: The American University, Washington College of Law, Arizona State University, Boston University, Cornell University, Emory University, Massachusetts Institute of Technology, Michigan State University, Pennsylvania State University, Syracuse University, University of California Davis, University of Maryland College Park, University of Minnesota, Humphrey School of Public Affairs, University of Minnesota - Law School, Vanderbilt University and Virginia Commonwealth University.

Placement at a specific university requested by a candidate cannot be arranged.

Level of Study: Fellowship for professionals

Application Deadline: Embassies and Commissions must submit their nominations to the Institute of International Education office in Washington, DC by October 1.

The deadlines for applicants vary by country.

If you are interested in applying for the Humphrey Fellowship Programme, please contact the U.S. Embassy or Fulbright Commission in your country.

Zawadi Africa Education Fund
Undergraduate Scholarship for Women
– in partnership with Google

The Zawadi Africa Education Fund is a programme designed to provide undergraduate scholarships to academically gifted girls from disadvantaged backgrounds in Africa to pursue higher education in the USA, Uganda, Ghana, South Africa, and Kenya.

The Zawadi Africa Education Fund is based on the highly successful Kennedy/Mboya Student airlifts of the 1960s, through a partnership with individuals and institutions with interest.

Girls who have suffered some form of abuse and are willing to further their education are usually given first attention - to become empowered. The scholarship covers an undergraduate degree in most ICT courses and Computer Engineering.

Application Deadline: From February to April yearly.
More details about the scholarship can be gotten
from the Zawadi Africa website.
http://www.zawadiafrica.org/apply-now/
Email: info@zawadiafrica.org

CHAPTER 2: JAPAN

Why study in Japan?

Japan is an economically developed country with visible advancements in technology. Both business organisations and schools strive to break grounds in other untapped areas to add to the country's growth. Japanese scientific technology and academic work are tools that support peoples' lives and societies all over the world.

The Japanese language and culture have its own uniqueness that provides a reason for being the way it is. It is such cultural origins that serve as the common foundation that links the people of the world together.

Studying in Japan provides not just an advanced and specialised knowledge, but opportunities to learn about Japanese language and culture as well. These multi-cultural experiences during your time of study will help you develop specific and essential skills.

Joint Japan/World Bank Graduate Scholarship Programme Japan

The World Bank and the Japanese government offer scholarships for the Master's Degree to students from developing countries. The programme covers all courses that are essential to development. The award is subject to enough funding from the government of Japan.

Level of Study: Master's degree

Application Deadline: Usually March 31

A full list of partner institutions and programmes offered can be found on the scholarship website: http://www.worldbank.org/scholarships and email: jjwbgsp@worldbank.org

CHAPTER 3: SWEDEN

Why study in Sweden?

It is a big step to study abroad, and the options are almost limitless. Therefore, what makes Sweden stand out as a study destination where Innovation and creativity run deep?

Sweden is a safe and modern country in Northern Europe, and it has accrued a spectacular reputation as an innovator and creative force. Sweden's famed corporate brands like; Volvo, IKEA, Ericsson, H&M and Saab - complement its cultural brands like; Ingmar Bergman, Abba, Astrid Lindgren, Bjorn Borg, August Strindberg, The Cardigans and Greta Garbo.

Swedish universities offer around 600 Master's degree programmes in English, ranging from Human Rights Law to mechanical engineering and can be structured in response to student demand. The result is a student-centric education system with open, informal relations between students and teachers, and where personal initiative and critical thought are prized.

Foreign students are welcome.

Many students studying in Sweden come from abroad, making up 8.5% of the student body, according to the Organisation for Economic Co-operation and Development (OECD), making Sweden is one of the world's most inclusive countries for education. But there is room for more; the number grew by over 80% over the last 4-year period. There are now PhD candidates from some 80 countries working towards their degrees in Sweden.

Sweden's educational policy is based on the recognition that a multicultural student body is a resource. Competition for places is keen, but students of all nationalities may apply, given the right credentials, and degree equivalency for past studies is granted on a flexible basis.

Scholarships are available

The Swedish Institute grants hundreds of awards every year to help foreign students make their stay in Sweden more afford-able. Currently, tuition fees for everyone are fully subsidised by the State. Sweden's public spending on education is the OECD's highest, at 4.9% of GDP. And because the cost of living is high in Sweden, International students can work while studying. Almost all Swedes speak English. Many Swedish companies use English as their official working language. Foreign students find that this prevalence of English helpful when adapting to their new sur-roundings.

Application and tuition fees apply to students who are not citizens of the EU, EEA, or Switzerland. However, the Swedish Government is ready to compensate these students with a gener-ous number of scholarships based on student need and academic merit. It is worthy to note that tuition-free education is available to students who enrol in PhD programmes.

The Swedish Institute and a significant number of Universities offer full and partial scholarships for international students in the form of tuition waivers.

PhD positions are usually offered as paid positions by universities or external funding bodies. This means that if you are offered a job as a PhD candidate, you will not pay fees and will receive a monthly salary.

Universities offer a range of different scholarship programmes for international students to help cover tuition fees or living costs. The specific scholarships on offer vary between universities. Visit your university's website directly or through www.google.com to find out more about available university scholarships and how to apply.

Source: studyinsweden.se

Why not make your choice?

University of Göteborg
International Office

Box 100, SE 405 30 Göteborg

Visiting address: Erik Dahlbergsgatan 11B

Phone: +46 (0) 31 773 53 28

Fax: +46 (0) 31 773 44 73

E-mail: internationalisering@gu.se

Website: http://www.gu.se/forskning/stipendier/gustipendier

Karlstads University
Universitetgatan 2, 651 88

Karlstads

Phone: +46 54-700 10 00

Fax: + 46 54-700 14 60

Email: information@kau.se

Website: http://www.kau.se/eng/

Linkoping University
International Office

SE 581 83 Linköping, Sweden

E-mail: intco@studc.liu.se

Website: http://www.liu.se/en

Stockholm University

International Office

SE-106 91, Stockholms, Sweden

E-mail: study@sb.su.se

Website: http://www.su.se

Karolinska Institute - A Medical University (Specialist)

Registry Office

SE-171 77, Stockholm

Fax: +46 831 110 1,

E-mail: registy@ki.se

Website: http://www.info.ki.se/ki/index_en.html

Royal Institute of Technology

SE-100 44, Stockholm, Sweden

E-mail: international@admin.kth.se

Swedish University of Agriculture

P.O. BOX 7070, SE-750 07, Uppsala, Sweden.

Fax: 46 18 67 20 00,

E-mail: registrator@slu.se

Website: http://www.slu.se/index_eng.cfm

University of Uppsala

P.O. BOX 256, SE-751 05, Uppsala, Sweden.

Fax: 46 18 471 16 00,

E-mail: interoff@uadm.uu.se

Website: http://www.uu.se

Lund University

International Office

SE-221 00, Lund, Sweden

Fax: 46 46 222 4111,

E-mail: desk@intsek.lu.se

Website: http://www.lu.se

Blekinge Institute of Technology

International Office

Head of International Office

Ms Maria Engelmark

Tel /Fax: 46 455 385202,

E-mail: maria.engelmark@bth.se

Website: http://www.bth.se/eng

Chalmers University of Technology

SE-41296, Goteborg, Sweden

Fax: 46 31 772 3872

Website: http://www.chalmers.se/en/

Dalarna University College

International Office,

Hgskolan Dalarna, 791 88, Falun Sweden

E-mail: ioffice@du.se

Website: http://www.du.se

Halmstad University

International Office

Box 823, SE-301 18, Halmstad, Sweden.

Fax: 46 35 14 8533,

E-mail: registator@hh.se

Website: http://www.hh.se/net/home

Jonkoping International Business School

Box 1026, 551 11, Jonkoping, Sweden.

Email: minna.Ryan-Ericsson@jibs.hj.se

Website: http://www.ihh.hj.se/eng/

Kristianstad University

International Office

291 88 Kristianstad Sweden

Fax: 44 12 96 51

Website: http://www.hkr.se

Lulea University of Technology

International Office

Fax: 46 920 49 29 57

Email: international.office@admin.luth.se

Website: http://www.ltu.se/eng/

Malmo University

International Office

Tel: 46 40 665 7260

E-mail: knut.bergknut@mah.se

Website: http://www.mah.se/english

Mid Sweden University

International Office

SE-851 70, Sundsvall Sweden.

Email: international@miun.se

Website: http://www.mh.se

Malardalen University

International Office

Email: international.office@mdh.se

Website: http://www.mdh.se/

Stockholm Institute of Education

International Office

Ms Ann Fridell

Email: ann.fridell@lhs.se

Website: http://www.lhs.se/english/

Stockholm University College of Physical Education

Box 5626, S-114 86, Stockholm, Sweden.

Fax: 46 84 022 280

Email: registrator@ihs.se

Website: http://www.his.se

Sophiahemmet University College, (specialised in Nursing)

Email: hogskolan@sophiahemmet.ki.se

CHAPTER 4: FINLAND

Why study in Finland?

Finland is another Nordic country in northern Europe, and a member of the EU - a magnificent country in which to study. Just like other Nordic nations, Finnish universities have no tuition fees for a regular degree. Student's education is subsidised by the State through the Ministry of Education. This arrangement also applies to international students. The only expenses students might incur during their stay are Union fees.

The Student Unions of the various universities, however, charge an annual Membership Fee to cover their activities. At multiple universities in Finland, the cost is about €70 each academic year. Student health care contribution is included, and an insurance fee applies. However, please note that the health care contribution is not health insurance; it allows students to use the student health care facilities provided by FSHS (Finnish Student Health Service). The Student Union membership is obligatory for undergraduate and postgraduate students (i.e. those studying for their Bachelor's or Master's degrees).

Postgraduate (Licentiate and PhD) students may join the Student Union if they wish. Student status, and especially the Student Union membership entitles learners to various services at affordable prices as well as an abundance of student discounts. Generally, students can work in Finland, although they stand a better chance when they have some knowledge of the Finnish and Swedish language.

There are currently no tuition fees charged in Finland, regardless of the level of studies and nationality of the student. However, tuition fees for non-EU/EEA students will be introduced from autumn 2017 onwards for English-taught Bachelor's or Master's programmes. Doctoral level studies will remain free of tuition fees.

Updates concerning the forthcoming non-EU tuition fees and related new scholarships options can be found at www.studyinfinland.fi/tuitionfees2017.

Remember that even when there are no tuition fees, you still need to plan your finances, you are expected to independently cover all your everyday living expenses during your studies in Finland.

Source: studyinfinland.fi

Scholarships are mainly available only for Doctoral level studies and research.

Åbo Akademi University

Academy of Fine Arts

Häme Polytechnic

Helsinki Business Polytechnic

Helsinki School of Economics University

Helsinki University of Technology

Lahti of Applied Sciences

Lappeenranta University of Technology

National Defense University

Oulu Institute of Technology

Satakunta Polytechnic

Sibelius Academy

Swedish School of Economics and Business Administration,

Finland Tampere Institute of Technology

Tampere University of Technology

Turku School of Economics

University of Art and Design Helsinki

University of Helsinki

University of Joensuu

University of Jyväskylä

University of Kuopio

University of Lapland

University of Oulu

University of Tampere

University of Turku

University of Vaasa

CHAPTER 5: NORWAY

Why study in Norway?

Norway offers you a unique student experience, and Norwegian institutions of higher education welcome applications sent by qualified students all over the world.

Internalisation is a priority within all sectors of the Norwegian education system, and universities and colleges are always working to facilitate international students. Nearly 12,000 foreign nationals are currently enrolled at Norwegian institutions of higher learning. International students may apply for admission to a variety of undergraduate and postgraduate degree programmes. You may go to Norway through established exchange programmes, an Institutional agreement or as a FREE MOVER where you arrange the stay (a type of study, length, and financing).

Tuition and Scholarship

Completing a university education is often considered to be an expensive endeavour, and the tuition fees often make up the bulk of the total expenses. Norwegian universities and state university colleges, as a rule, do not charge tuition fees for international students. "Nothing is really free" is a saying that is true for most cases, but in Norway, it is possible to get a quality education without having to pay tuition. Also, if specific prerequisites are met, you could be eligible for financial support that can pay for your living expenses. Through the various fellowship programmes, scholarship schemes or student loans, international students can receive funding for a full degree programme.

Admission and Application

To obtain the necessary application form and the information about the application deadlines, you will have to contact each university or college. In general, the application deadline for foreign students is between January 15 to March 15 for courses starting the following autumn (August). Please note that some institutions have a separate, earlier pre-qualification deadline.

The following are a list of Institutions in Norway:

Norwegian University of Life Sciences (UMB)

Norwegian University of Science and Technology (NTNU)

University of Agder (UiA)

University of Bergen (UiB)

University of Oslo (UiO)

University of Stavanger (UiS)

University of Tromsø (UiT)

Specialised University Institutions

MF Norwegian School of Theology

Norwegian Academy of Music (NMH)

Norwegian School of Sport Sciences (NIH)

Norwegian School of Veterinary Science.

Visit www.studyinnorway.no for more information.

CHAPTER 6: GERMANY

Why study in Germany?

Germany is the third most popular destination for international students in the world, and one of the economic powers in Europe. More than twelve per cent of students in German universities come from abroad. Germany is an attractive place to study and has a lot to offer to international students, with a diverse range of activities and places of interests from cultural and historic buildings, towns, and winter sports areas, including the seas and beaches.

German university degrees are highly recognised by employers worldwide. Due to its technological advancement and research facilities. It's engineering universities rank amongst the best in the world, and these institutions are strategically close to the country's industrial centres for practical interaction purposes.

As of October 2014, all Universities in Germany will not charge any tuition fees for undergraduate studies for all students, including international students. In some Federal States, universities will charge a semester contribution (about 50 Euros) and/or administration fees (about 50 Euros).

Unlike undergraduate studies, most Master's studies in Germany come with tuition fees, but they're not as high as in other countries.

PhD students are charged tuition only after completing their first six semesters and must pay a semester contribution of approximately 150-200 euros. Doctoral students usually work on a research project (paid PhD position) or receive a scholarship.

Cost of studying in Germany

On average, national & EU students spend about 850 Euros per month to cover for accommodation, transport, food, and miscellaneous expenses. Rent (housing) usually requires the most financial input.

CHAPTER 7: DENMARK

Why study in Denmark?

Until recently, Denmark was the home of free education. Several Danish Institutions offer a scholarship programme and tuition waivers for International Students. The tuition-free education for international students now only applies to EU/EAA nationals; they do not pay application fees either. Denmark is one of the safest and friendliest countries that guarantees Individual freedom, freedom of speech, equal rights, and possibilities for everyone.

The Danish legislation ensures religious freedom for all citizens and prevents discrimination by gender, race, or sexual orientation. Furthermore, the educational system and everyday life in Denmark offer an understanding of its Scandinavian history, culture, and politics, promoting solidarity, respect and tolerance – the central values in the democratic Scandinavian societies. Free Health Insurance gives all international students the right to free medical service.

One university that offers a tuition fee waiver and other scholarship programmes are:

Aalborg University

If you are a non-EU citizen, your application will be considered as soon as an application fee of 10 5euros is received, which is refundable if you are admitted. A bank transfer fee and or cheque payment is deducted from your application fee before reimbursement. If you apply for more than one programme, you will only need to pay the application fee once and use the receipt for each other programme application.

If you hold a Bachelor's Degree from a university outside of the EU, you must submit an official document that states that your qualification is the equivalent of a full Danish Bachelor degree or a First Cycle Degree according to the Framework for the European Higher Education Area - Bologna Framework.

Tuition Waivers at Aalborg University

The tuition waiver is politically decided, and it is not possible to apply for it. The exemption will cover tuition fees for the whole period of study (2 years) and is only for students who are subject to tuition fees (non-European students without a permanent residence permit for Denmark). The waiver does not cover living costs or any other expenses.

When you apply for a Master's programme, you are automatically considered if you fulfil the criteria. However, meeting such standards does not guarantee you a tuition waiver – it only means you are eligible to be considered for one, and you must apply for a Master´s programme before the 1st of April.

For more information, please visit: http://www.en.aau.dk/

INNO+ Scholarship at Aalborg University

Some INNO+ 2-year Masters level scholarships in Medicine with Industrial Specialization are available at Aalborg University.

For more information, please check http://www.smh.aau.dk/INNO-Scholarship+/

Some INNO+ 2-year Masters level scholarships in Global Systems Design (Copenhagen) are available at Aalborg University.

For more information, please check http://www.et.aau.dk/

department/jobs-and-scholarships/

Who Can Receive INNO+ Scholarship? The scholarships will be awarded to top-class students preferably from Brazil, India, China, South Korea, the USA, and Japan.

CHAPTER 8: UNITED KINGDOM

Why study in the United Kingdom?

The UK might be small, but it has many places to study and a popular study haven for international students. It should be noted that some universities in the UK are historical and many were built in the 19th century. British universities are highly ranked, and their educational qualifications accepted across the world. Most UK Universities offers various full- and partly- sponsored Scholarships for international students, and many are from Africa, and other underdeveloped war-torn countries. These scholarships cover both undergraduate, postgraduate and PhD degrees.

Oxford University

Oxford University, one of the oldest world-leading institution and offers a full scholarship to students from developing countries. The awards are usually financed by undergraduates (jointly with colleges and university) and cover both university and college fees, return air travel, as well as maintenance for the duration of studies. No funding is provided for spouses and dependents.

The Reach Oxford concept.

Scholarships are for students from low-income countries and developing countries (formerly Oxford Students Scholarship). To apply for Reach Oxford, students must complete a separate application form available at www.admin.ox.ac.uk/io/ or by emailing the International Office at international. office@admin.ox.ac.uk

Shell Centenary Scholarship
for Postgraduates

The Shell Centenary scholarships are funded by the Shell Centenary Scholarship Fund (TSCSF) and the University of Oxford. Some awards are also jointly funded with the UK Foreign and Commonwealth Office and are known as the Shell Centenary Chevening Scholarships.

Commonwealth Shared
Scholarship Scheme (CSSS)

The Commonwealth Shared Scholarships represent a unique partnership between the UK government and many British Universities. Awards made under this scheme are jointly funded by the Department for International Development (DFID) as part of the British International Development programme for developing countries, and the University of Oxford. The scheme is administered by the Commonwealth Scholarship Commission (CSC), whose secretariat is provided by the Association of Commonwealth Universities (ACU) in London. For more information, contact: www.admin.ox.ac.uk/io/

Clarendon Scholarship,
University of Oxford

Like all fully funded Oxford scholarships, the Clarendon Scholarship covers tuition and college fees and offers a generous grant for living costs. However, Clarendon's further appeal lies in its unique community of scholars.

As well as providing for fees and living costs, Clarendon aims to enhance the Oxford experience, and the Scholars' Association is active in giving events which range from the academic and educational, via the career-oriented, to the cultural and social.

For more information, please visit http://www.ox.ac.uk/

Westminster Full International Scholarship

There are several full scholarships for international students, especially those from developing, and war-torn countries. These scholarships mostly cover undergraduate and postgraduate students and usually run between March and May of every year. Please check the website for a full list of countries covered under this scholarship scheme.

https://www.westminster.ac.uk/study/prospective-students/ fees-and-funding/scholarships/ international-undergraduate-scholarships/Westminster-full-international-scholarship.

Gates Cambridge Scholarship Programme

Citizens of any country outside the United Kingdom can apply for full-time residential courses of study at the University of Cambridge.

The Gates Cambridge Scholarship covers the full cost of studying and includes airfare and visa costs, fieldwork, and a family allowance.

For more information, please visit the Gates Cambridge website: https://www.gatescambridge.org

Other UK Universities that run annual Scholarship Programmes for International Students are:

The Universities of London, Brighton, Edinburgh, Hull, Leeds, Birmingham, Kingston, Kent, Manchester Metropolitan University and University Business School.

CHAPTER 9: AUSTRIA

Why study in Austria?

It may be relatively small, but there are many reasons to study in Austria, including some universities which rank among the world's best. In terms of area, Austria is no more significant than the US State of Maine, and in terms of population, it is home to roughly the same number of people as the UK's capital, London. Furthermore, this beautiful Central European country is, full of stunning landscapes and exuberant cities and should not be judged just by its size.

This is the country that brought the world great composers such as Wolfgang Amadeus Mozart, and innovative thinkers such as Sigmund Freud and Ludwig Wittgenstein, and the iconic musical, The Sound of Music. Who can forget the equally memorable one-liners of the Austrian-born actor-turned-politician Arnold Schwarzenegger?

If you are a non-EU/EEA student, federal/public universities in Austria only charge about 363.36 Euros to 726.72 Euros per semester for tuition fees plus 19.20 Euros for the Student Union membership fee and 50 Euros insurance fee per semester. If you are a citizen of a least developed country, you may be exempted from tuition fees at public universities in Austria and only need to pay the Student Union membership fee and insurance.

Cost of Studying in Austria

The cost of living for students in Austria is approximately

900-1300 Euros per month to cover accommodation, food, and personal expenses.

CHAPTER 10: AUSTRALIA

Why study in Australia?

When Australia is mentioned, most people imagine wide bushy spaces, kangaroos, koalas and clean air and water. Australia, however, has more to offer than just that! Many international students choose to study in Australia because of its friendly, laid-back nature, excellent education system, and a high standard of living. Australia is the third most popular destination for international students in the English- speaking world because of its cultural diversity, friendly citizens, and high-quality education.

Cost of Living

Australia's standard of living is amongst the highest in the world. However, living expenses and tuition costs are considerably lower in Australia than in the United States and the United Kingdom. International students can take jobs (up to 20 hours per week). Scholarships are also available.

Technology

The quality of scientific research is another appeal – the country is at the forefront of new technology and innovations.

Endeavour Postgraduate Awards

This Scholarship provides financial support for international applicants to undertake a Masters or PhD level degree either by coursework or research in any field for up to four years.

The detailed list of all the target countries under this scholarship can be viewed on the site listed below:

http://www.scholars4dev.com/3710/endeavour-postgraduate-scholarship-awards/

Scholarship value/inclusions/duration.

The scholarship value is up to $272,500 (PhD) and $140,500 (Masters). It includes travel allowance, housing allowance, monthly stipends, health, and travel insurance.

Recipients will also receive tuition fees paid up to the maximum study/research duration, which includes student service and amenities fees.

The duration of the scholarship is up to 2 years for a Masters and up to 4 years for a PhD.

Email: endeavour@education.gov.au

https://internationaleducation.gov.au/Endeavour%20programme/Scholarships-and-Fellowships/Pages/default.aspx.

Griffith University, Nathan

Griffith International offers scholarships valued at $5,000 each to outstanding international high school graduates applying for undergraduate studies at Griffith University.

Postgraduate Excellence Scholarships are valued at $3,000 each for outstanding international students. Two payments of $1,500 will be made towards each recipient's tuition fees in the first and second semester of the first year of their programme.

Details of various scholarship programmes offered by Griffith

University for international students are on the University websites:

https://www.griffith.edu.au/international/scholarships-finance/scholarships-awards/griffith-university-funded-scholarships-and-awards

and

https://www.griffith.edu.au/international/scholarships-finance/scholarships-awards/ externally-funded-scholarships-and-awards.

Queensland University of Technology, Brisbane

Australian Government Research Training Programme (RTP) Stipend (International) is awarded by the Australian government to encourage exceptional students to undertake research degrees in Australia.

According to www.qut.edu.au, the scholarship is indexed annually ($27,082 in 2018) and covers tax exemption and living costs for up to two years for a Masters student and 3 years for a PhD and doctoral students.

Eligibility is strictly on academic performance and covers most faculties in the university such as Business, Creative Industries, Education, Health, Law, Science and the Engineering, Institute of Health and Biomedical Innovation (IHBI), the Institute for Future Environments. The scholarship covers tuition, health and living expenses. However, students should not receive income from another source to support general living costs if that income is higher than 75% of the RTP stipend.

QUT also has undergraduate scholarships with emphasis on women, sporting excellence and equity (more details are on the website).

Email: research.scholarships@qut.edu.au

https://www.qut.edu.au/study/fees-and-scholarships/scholarships-and-prizes/international-postgraduate-research-scholarship-iprs

The University of Adelaide

The University of Adelaide offers scholarships for international students wishing to study in Australia.

University of Melbourne, Parkville

The Melbourne Scholarships Programme is one of the most generous of its kind in Australia. The programme spans both undergraduate and postgraduate courses with benefits ranging from fee relief to payments to assist with living, study, and travel expenses.

Some scholarships are awarded purely on academic merit and others on a mixture of academic ability and equity issues.

Full details are on the University website.

https://futurestudents.unimelb.edu.au/admissions/scholarships/undergraduate_ scholarships_for_international_students

https://futurestudents.unimelb.edu.au/admissions/scholarships/graduate_scholarships_for_ international students.

CHAPTER 11:
SOUTH AFRICA

Why study in South Africa?

If you want to experience life in one of the most diverse and complex countries in the world, you may choose to study in South Africa. Since the 1990s, following legislation to overturn decades of enforced racial segregation, the state is nicknamed the "Rainbow Nation" in recognition of its unique multicultural character.

Universities in South Africa

If you study in South Africa at the undergraduate level, it will usually take three years of full-time study to complete a Bachelor's Degree, and one or two years to complete a Master's Degree.

As in countries such as Australia and New Zealand, those who study in South Africa do not receive an overall grade for their bachelor's degree with a level of honours (such as 2:1 or 1st). Instead, after their third year of study, students have the option to either graduate with a Bachelor's Degree Certificate or take a further one-year Honours Course to get their Honours Certification. This is an extra postgraduate year of study in which a research thesis must be completed in the same area of education as the student's Bachelor's Degree.

Most universities in South Africa offer multicultural student communities, excellent academic facilities, a range of social activities and clubs, and good support systems for international students.

Monash Scholarship

Monash scholarships provide learning opportunities for the highest achieving students. Scholarships are offered to students to encourage and reward academic excellence in previous studies.

Monash South Africa offers scholarships for South African and International students pursuing undergraduate programmes. Applicants must be enrolled or have received an offer as a full-time student at Monash South Africa in an undergraduate course of study.

https://www.msa.ac.za/study/scholarships-bursaries/

Tel: +27 11 950 4000, +27 11 950 4009

CHAPTER 12: THE UNITED ARAB EMIRATES

Why study in the UAE?

The United Arab Emirates (UAE) is positioned strategically within a five-hour flight away from half of the world's population, bringing Asia to the rest of the world, with the government investing significantly in infrastructure, and due to its zero tax payment, has made the country popular amongst many business/companies.

With the local airports; Emirates, Etihad, and Air Arabia airlines, it is easy to find a flight home when the university holidays come.

The UAE is one of the best places to live in the Middle East. An open and tolerant society, coupled with one of the lowest crime rates worldwide, many students have made this a destination of choice. Furthermore, the government has ensured the highest quality of education and healthcare facilities and has been successful in attracting many cultural performances, sporting, and entertainment events, and houses the world's best museums. The dedicated cultural district of Saadiyat Island will be home to new branches opened by internationally renowned museums such as New York's Guggenheim and Paris' Louvre and alongside is the planned Sheikh Zayed Museum, designed by Norman Foster that gives the United Arab Emirate a unique multicultural hub.

The UAE also attracts international institutions and is home to the International Renewable Energy Agency (IRENA) and the CNN Middle East regional headquarters.

Abu Dhabi is moving from an oil-based economy to one driven by innovation and knowledge. Internationally recognised institutions are invited to support the nation's economic development.

Leading universities offer programmes or have set up branch university campuses in Abu Dhabi, and Dubai, including INSEAD, the Massachusetts Institute of Technology, New York University, and Paris- Sorbonne.

The Masdar Institute of Science and Technology

The Institute offers cutting-edge research focused on advanced energy and sustainable technology, working in collaboration with MIT - a sustainable campus with state-of-the-art facilities and equipment and full scholarships that include a competitive stipend and a multicultural environment with students from more than 60 countries.

There are four scholarships available to applicants of Masdar Institute viz. the Masdar Institute Scholarship, IRENA Scholarship, Toyota Scholarship, and the ICT Fund Scholarship.

Qualified Master's and Doctorate degree applicants to Masdar Institute will receive full scholarship benefits upon admission.

The Masdar Institute Scholarship benefits include the following:

- 100% of all tuition fees
- All required textbooks
- A laptop
- Reimbursement of GRE and TOEFL exam/test fees
- Masdar Institute housing
- Monthly stipend
- Health insurance

- Annual return ticket home (if applicable)

Note: High grades and scores are a prerequisite but do not guarantee admission. Admission standards are by those of the Massachusetts Institute of Technology (MIT).

For requirements and details of the other scholarships, please visit the MASDAR scholarship website: https://masdar.ac.ae/admissions/scholarships

CHAPTER 13: CANADA

Why study in Canada?

With one of the longest coastlines, vast wilderness, world-class cities, and a culture of tolerance and diversity, Canada is a natural destination for thousands of international students. Maybe you don't know much about Canada beyond its ski slopes and wild moose population, but there are plenty of reasons why you should study in this amazing country. Canadia's high-quality education comes at an affordable cost and offers safe communities, high-tech campuses, rich multiculturalism and finally, the possibility of easy immigration at the end of your studies.

There are no tuition-free universities or colleges in Canada, but the fees are comparatively cheaper than in other countries. Also, many universities and colleges offer scholarships to international students.

According to www.canada.ca, international students can work on-campus without a work permit provided they are full-time, post-secondary students at recognised public or private schools, have a valid study permit, and have a Social Insurance Number. Students must stop working on campus on the day they are no longer studying full time, or their study permit expires. Working off-campus as an international student in Canada has more stringent criteria listed in www.canada.ca.

Humber International Entrance Scholarships

Humber offers full and partial renewable scholarships to new international undergraduate classes in January and September of every year in Toronto, Canada. Students can take undergraduate programmes offered at the college - visit www.humber.ca

Scholarships depend on the discretion of the institution in a particular year. For example, two full-tuition scholarships were awarded, and two $5,000 scholarships were available in September 2017. One full-tuition scholarship and one $5,000 scholarship will be available in January 2019, and seven $5000 awards and two $3000 scholarships will be available in September 2019. The awards are renewable for students who maintain a minimum average of 75%.

For full details on how to apply for the scholarship, visit the official scholarship website at http://international.humber.ca/study-at-humber/scholarships.html

Vanier Canada Graduate Scholarships

The awards were created to attract and retain world-class doctoral students and to establish Canada as a global centre of excellence in research and higher learning. The scholarships are towards a doctoral degree (or combined MA/PhD or MD/PhD).

Up to 167 scholarships are awarded annually to Canadian citizens, permanent residents of Canada and foreign students to take PhD programmes (or combined MA/PhD or MD/PhD) in health research, natural sciences and/or engineering research; and social sciences and/or humanities research.

The scholarships are worth $50,000 per year for three years. To be considered for the awards, an applicant must be nominated by one Canadian institution that received a Vanier CGS quota. (See 2015-2018 Vanier CGS Quota Memo for Institutions at www.vanier.gc.ca). Also, interested applicants must be pursuing a first doctoral degree (including a joint undergraduate/graduate research programme such as MD/PhD, DVM/PhD, JD/PhD[1] – if it has a significant research component). Interested applicants must intend to pursue, in the summer semester or the academic year following the announcement of results, full-time doctoral (or a joint graduate programme such as MD/PhD, DVM/PhD, JD/PhD) studies and research at the nominating institution.

- Applicants must not have completed more than 20-months of doctoral studies as of May 1, 2019
- She/he must have achieved a first-class average (as determined by their institution) in each of the last two years of full-time study or equivalent
- He/she must not hold, or have held, a doctoral-level scholarship or fellowship from the Canadian Institutes of Health Research (CIHR), Natural Sciences and Engineering Research Council (NSERC) or Social Sciences and Humanities Research Council (SSHRC), to undertake a doctoral degree.

Candidates must be nominated by a Canadian Institution with a level at which they want to study. Candidates cannot apply directly to the Vanier CGS programme. This can be initiated in one of two ways: either the student informs the faculty of graduate studies at the selected institution of their intent to apply to the Vanier CGS programme or the institution initiates the nomination process by contacting the desired candidate.

For further information on the application, visit the official scholarship website at www.vanier.gc.ca. Only the PhD portion of a combined degree is eligible for funding and candidates are encouraged to contact the institution for its definition of a first-class average.

CHAPTER 14: TURKEY

Why study in Turkey?

Turkey has a unique strategic position at the crossroads of East and West, which endows this country with nearly ten-thousand years of history. As part of Asia and part of Europe, Turkey has remarkably wide climatic and geographical variations. Due to its location, surrounded by seas on three sides, Turkey has always been the centre of trade from the Silk Road and spice routes. Today, even in the most inaccessible or isolated corners, one can quickly feel and see the traces of different cultures. As the Turkish landscape encompasses a vast variety of geographical zone, it has the combined characteristics of the three continents of the world: Europe, Africa and Asia.

Turkish Universities provide:

- High standards of education

The quality of the training and teaching staff at Turkish Universities offers you a world of opportunities to get the skills you will need for a global society.

- Internationally recognised degrees

For further information on degree recognition, you can consult with your country's educational authorities.

- Modern campuses with outstanding facilities

You will find libraries and advanced laboratories in which you can search for and acquire knowledge. With sports and cultural facilities, student clubs and dormitories - you will enjoy being a student in Turkey.

- Cultural diversity

Diversity is richness. You will meet East and West together in Turkey, which has the combined characteristics of the two continents: Europe and Asia. You will not be a foreigner in Turkey because it is a mosaic of cultures.

- Safe and affordable education

Turkey is a place where you can find affordable education. Tuition and cost of living are lower than in most European countries and the U.S. However, international students have no legal rights to work in either private or public offices.

- A warm and friendly environment

As a young nation (31% of the Turkish population are between the ages of 12-24) Turkey welcomes young people. Turkish people are traditionally very hospitable.

In Turkey, students will have the opportunity to experience both modernity and tradition in one of the safest and most stable countries in the region. Furthermore, in some Turkish Universities, the language of instruction is English, and others give opportunities to learn English. Above all, the high quality of education will prepare students for the future.

Turkiye Scholarships

The Turkiye Scholarships are open to international candidates from any country other than Turkey. And each scholarship includes a university placement. This means that applicants will be placed in a university and programme that suits their preferences specified in the online application form. The awards are open to graduate students, or students that are able to graduate at the end of the current academic year, looking to possess a Bachelor's, Master's, or PhD degree.

The Turkiye Scholarships is divided into rounds where countries are grouped, and candidates from the specified countries can apply only during these rounds.

To get further details on the Turkiye Scholarships; scholarship value, the eligible countries, the rounds, and deadlines visit the website: www.turkiyeburslari.gov.tr

CHAPTER 15: NEW ZEALAND

Why study in New Zealand?

New Zealand has so much to offer students - a fantastic place to learn English, and the most beautiful country in the world. Explore the country and experience something new while you study. New Zealanders are friendly and welcoming towards international students.

There are so many activities – adventure and cultural – to experience while making friends from around the world. You can enjoy fantastic scenery and enjoy activities that you've ever dreamed of doing.

Travel

Tourism is a popular attraction in this small, safe, and peaceful country (4.7m people) that is renowned for its magnificent scenic countryside, adventure experiences, cultural activities, and friendly, welcoming people. The New Zealand Tourism site will give you an idea of what's on offer. Study during the week and choose activities like bungee jumping, skiing, hiking, rafting, or exploring local culture in your free time. You might prefer to shop at a local market, visit a museum, or meet with friends at a local café – it's your choice.

Work

Many students can work up to 20 hours per week if they have a Student Visa. Working Holiday Visa holders can also study a short course of English as part of the New Zealand experience.

New Zealand Development Scholarships

The New Zealand Development Scholarships (NZDS), funded by the New Zealand Aid Programme, offers academic opportunities to international students from selected countries in Africa, Asia, Latin America, and the Caribbean to gain knowledge through post-graduate studies in some New Zealand universities and institutes of technology. The scholarships include tuition fees, travel costs, living allowance, and insurance.

Depending on the country the candidate is from, the scholarships are available for the following levels: Postgraduate Certificate (6 months), Postgraduate Diploma (1 year), Master's Degree (1-2 years), or PhD (up to 3 years and 6 months).

Fields of study are those that are relevant to the development needs of the candidate's country (i.e. renewable energy, agriculture development, disaster risk management, private and public sector development). Find out the preferred courses for specific countries at www.mfat.govt.nz

The scholarships are targeted at citizens of selected countries in Africa, Asia, Latin America, and the Caribbean - www.mfat.govt.nz

The awards include full tuition fees, a living allowance (NZ$480 per week), an establishment allowance (NZ$3000), medical and travel insurance, pastoral and academic support at the institution, and assistance with research and thesis costs for most postgraduate research students.

For eligibility criteria and application instructions, visit www.mfat.govt.mz/en/aid-and-development/scholarships/types-of-scholarships

The UC International First
Year Scholarships

Offered by the University of Canterbury, the scholarship is open to top-achieving international students commencing an undergraduate degree programme at the University. Up to 25 scholarships may be awarded and are targeted at international students from any country except New Zealand and Australia.

The duration is for one year and is valued at
$10,000, $15,000, or $20,000.

Visit www.canterbury.ac.nz/scholarshipsearch
for detailed information.

CHAPTER 16: CHINA

Why study in China?

Studying abroad in China allows international students to view things from the Chinese perspective. Merging knowledge from both China and their home countries will give students an advantage to explore potential opportunities in China. Because of its long history and rich culture, China has become one of the most famous destinations for international students.

International students can learn and save money while studying in China. Both living costs and school fees are comparatively inexpensive, especially in comparison with the United States and other western countries. There are scholarships from the government, universities, foundations, and corporations designed to support international students from different academic disciplines. International students are now allowed to work part-time or take on internships while they are studying. International students in China with a residence permit can take part-time jobs or courses outside the campus as long as they obtain approval from their academic institutions and the entry and exit administrative authorities.

China is a unified multi-ethnic country jointly created by the people of all 56 ethnic groups. In the long course of its evolution, people of all 56 ethnic groups in China have maintained close contacts, developed interdependently, communicated and fused with one another, and stood together through weal and woe, forming today's unified multi-ethnic Chinese nation, and promoting the development of the country and social progress.

The Chinese Government Scholarship
- Great Wall Programme

The Great Wall Programme is a full scholarship established by the Chinese Ministry of Education for the United Nations Educational, Scientific and Cultural Organization (UNESCO) to sponsor students and scholars in developing countries to study and conduct research in China. This programme only supports general scholars and senior scholars.

Scholarship recipients who are admitted into Chinese-taught programmes and who are without adequate Chinese proficiency are required to get the approval from both CSC and UNESCO for one academic year of Chinese language study.

This scholarship covers, in general, one academic year of study and covers tuition waiver, accommodation, stipend, and comprehensive medical insurance. UNESCO covers international travel fare, a monthly pocket allowance and a termination allowance.

CHAPTER 17: TAIWAN

Why study in Taiwan?

Taiwan has an outstanding higher education system that provides opportunities for international students to study a wide variety of subjects, ranging from the Chinese language and history to tropical agriculture and forestry, genetic engineering, business, semiconductors and more. Chinese culture holds education and scholarship in high regard, and nowhere is this truer than in Taiwan where you will experience a vibrant, modern society rooted in one of the world's most ancient cultures and populated by some of the most friendly and hospitable people on the planet. There are many reasons international students will find Taiwan an exciting and rewarding place to pursue their education viz:

- The high quality of academic resources
- A vibrant and colourful culture
- As a successful student, you have an increased chance of getting a job back in your home country

International students in Taiwan can apply for work permits for employment as they learn. However, these students can only work for a maximum of 16 hours a week. The work permit is valid for 6 months, after which the student can apply for a renewal.

Taiwan Government Scholarships

The scholarships are open for international students seeking Bachelors, Masters, or PhD degrees in Taiwan colleges and universities participating in the scholarship programme. For a list of these universities and colleges, visit www.english.moe.gov.tw

The scholarship has two parts:

- Tuition and payment of academic fees, including credit fee. Upon the validation of tuition and fees, the Ministry of Education awards each recipient up to NTD40,000 per semester. However, if the total amount of these fees should exceed NTD40,000, the remainder of all costs shall be covered by either the recipient or the recipient's college
- Subsistence allowance: The Ministry of Education offers each recipient undertaking undergraduate studies a monthly stipend of NTD15,000 and offers each recipient taking postgraduate studies a monthly stipend of NTD20,000.
- Tuition and academic fees do not include administration fees, thesis costs, advising fees, insurance premiums, accommodation, internet access - all of which are payable by the student

The maximum period of each scholarship is four years for undergraduate programmes, two years for Masters programmes, and four years for Doctorates. The maximum length of the total awards for each recipient is five years.

For information on eligibility criteria and further application instructions, visit www.edu.law.moe.gov.tw

CHAPTER 18: THE NETHERLANDS

Why study in The Netherlands?

With the number of study destinations increasing annually, there are many reasons why the increasingly popular Netherlands should make your shortlist.

The Netherlands, or less formally Holland, was the first non-English speaking country to offer courses and degrees in English back in the 1950s. This experience along with a unique teaching approach involving more teamwork and problem-solving compared to other countries has helped Holland become one of the leading alternative destinations after studying in the UK, Australia, and the USA.

The Netherlands (Holland) is in North-west Europe across the sea from the UK and with borders to Belgium and Germany. It is easy to visit other countries during your studies as extensive transport links by aeroplane, train and bus to most European countries exist. Many people in the country speak English as well as their native Dutch language. You will also find the Dutch people very welcoming and happy to help you with your travels.

Education in the Netherlands is intensive, and while in some circumstances, you may be able to complete some part-time work you should expect to commit most of your time to your studies.

According to www.studyinholland.nl, students from Switzerland, Croatia, and EU/EEA countries can work without restrictions. However, other students require a work permit and can only work for a maximum of 16 hours a week or full-time during the summer months of June, July, and August.

However, students studying at the Dutch host institution and who are required to do an internship as part of their programme, do not need a work permit. The host institution and employer would need to sign an internship agreement.

Holland Scholarship for Non-EEA International Students

The Holland Scholarship, financed by the Dutch Ministry of Education, Culture and Science, is for international students outside the European Economic Area (EEA) who want to do their bachelor's or a Master's at one of the Dutch research universities of applied sciences in Holland.

The scholarship amounts to €5,000. Please note that this is not a full-tuition scholarship. The grant is awarded for one year and can only be received once.

Further information about the application procedure and the specific deadlines are available on the website of the institution of your choice. It is essential to visit the official website (link found below) for detailed information on how to apply for this scholarship.

Official Scholarship Website: http://www.studyinholland.nl/scholarships/holland-scholarship

World Citizen Talent Scholarships for International Students

Every year, The Hague University of Applied Sciences offers 3 (one-time) scholarships available to prospective Master's degree students who are young, intelligent, talented, and ambitious. These students must not be citizens of or live in The Netherlands.

Each scholarship is worth €5,000.

To apply for the scholarship, applicants must first apply for a Master Programme and write an essay following the essay guidelines on:

www.thehagueuniversity.com/study-choice/admissions-and-finances/financing-your-bachelor-study/scholarships/essay-guidelines.

Further information on the application procedure and eligibility criteria can be obtained on www.thehagueuniversity.com.

CHAPTER 19: BELGIUM

Why study in Belgium?

There are many reasons to study at a world-renowned university in Belgium. Students will have excellent opportunities for international networking, being part of famous multicultural and multilingual cities, enjoying a host of regional cuisines and specialities, visiting the beautiful countryside, and experiencing an overall high quality of life, and, of course, those delicious Belgian waffles.

An established hub for international politics, Belgium's capital Brussels has even more ambassadors and journalists than Washington DC and is the headquarters of many international businesses and organisations. Furthermore, Belgium's resident population is also highly global, with around a quarter of the people of 11 million known as 'new Belgians' – those from other countries, and their descendants, who have become permanent citizens.

In Expatica's guide for students seeking to study in Belgium, it states that foreign students enrolled at a Belgian institution and have valid residence permit can work up to 20 hours a week as long as it does not interfere with their studies. Students will need to get a written fixed term contract from their employer, which is known as a "student employment contract," and a type C work permit.

VLIR-UOS Training and Masters Scholarships in Belgium

VLIR-UOS awards scholarships to students from 31 eligible countries in Africa, Asia, and Latin-America, to follow an English-taught training or Masters programmes at a Flemish university or university college in Belgium. For a list of universities, visit www.vliruos.be.

This scholarship is targeted at students from the following countries:

Africa – Benin, Burkina Faso, Burundi, DR Congo, Ethiopia, Guinea, Cameroun, Kenya, Madagascar, Mali, Morocco, Mozambique, Niger, Rwanda, Senegal, South Africa, Tanzania, Uganda, Zimbabwe.

Asia – Cambodia, Indonesia, Philippines, Palestinian Territories, Vietnam.

Latin America – Bolivia, Cuba, Ecuador, Guatemala, Haiti, Nicaragua, Peru.

VLIR-UOS only provide full scholarships for the total duration of the training or Masters degree. The scholarships cover allowance, accommodation, insurance, international travel, and tuition. Read more at www.vliruos.be.

To apply for this scholarship, candidates must enrol for the Master's programme. Applications submitted directly to VLIR-UOS will not be considered. Also, the deadline for the award varies and is determined by the Masters or Training programme.

For more information on the application procedure and eligibility criteria, check the official website: www.vliruos.be.

Science@Leuven Scholarships
for International Students

The K.U. Leuven Faculty of Science offers this scholarship to motivated and talented international students who are interested in participating in a Masters programme at the Katholieke Universiteit Leuven.

The scholarship can be valued for up to €10,000 for 1 year and covers the tuition fee, insurance, and health insurance. Amounts awarded for living expenses can vary.

For a two-year Master's programme, the scholarship for the second Masters year will be extended if the student had outstanding results in the first year.

Note: Only applications that have been submitted (with the International Office and registered on the website of the scholarship) before the 15th of February will be considered for the award.

To get information on eligibility criteria and application procedure, check out the official scholarship website: http://wet.kuleuven.be/english.

CHAPTER 20: SWITZERLAND

Why study in Switzerland?

Switzerland is an excellent location for living, studying, and working. Its cultural variety, beautiful landscape, and innovative environment offer first-class surroundings for both personal well-being and career advancement.

The country is one of the most competitive in the world and widely recognised internationally as a centre of excellence in education, research, and innovation. Great emphasis is placed on ensuring the autonomy of Swiss universities and researchers, on fostering competition and quality, and encouraging a broad-minded outlook.

Switzerland's small size has favoured the emergence of well-developed research and development networks, whose expertise is continuously implemented in the economy and society. At the same time, Switzerland is part of the global community and maintains a worldwide network of corporations and partnerships in education and science.

According to www.educations.com, students who have obtained a residence permit and proven to have financial resources necessary for their studies can take a job as long as the university issued a statement confirming that the employment will not prolong the length of the study programme.

For foreign students, the work hours are limited to 15 per week.

However, this is flexible - depending on the canton. For example, in Geneva, a student can work up to 30 hours per week.

Swiss Government Excellence Scholarships for Foreign Students

Each year, the Swiss Confederation awards Government Excellence Scholarships to promote international exchange and research cooperation between Switzerland and over 180 other countries.

The research scholarship is available to post-graduate researchers in any discipline (who hold a master's degree as a minimum) who are planning to come to Switzerland to pursue research or further studies at doctoral or post-doctoral level in one of the 10 Swiss cantonal universities, the two Swiss federal institutes of technology or public teaching and research institutes.

The scholarship covers a monthly payment, exemption of tuition fees, health insurance, airfare, and a housing allowance as applicable. Please refer to the country-specific fact sheets for specific scholarship benefits.

It is essential to visit the official website (link found below) for detailed information on how to apply for this scholarship. Also, for eligibility criteria, refer to the canton-specific fact sheets for general and specific eligibility criteria.

Official Scholarship Website: www.sbfi.admin.ch/
scholarships_eng

The University of Lausanne Master's Grants in Switzerland for Foreign Students

The University of Lausanne, Switzerland offers this Master's Grant on a competitive basis to international students who seek to pursue a Master's Degree at the University.

Fields of study include all Master's programmes offered by the university (refer to www.unil.ch) except a Masters from the School of Medicine, Law from the Universities of Zurich and Lausanne, Education, Criminal Law, Magistracy Specialism, and all MASs (PhD programmes).

The scholarship is granted for the minimum statutory period of the programme chosen by the student. It amounts to CHF 1,600 per month from 15 September to 15 July (or 10 months a year) for the complete duration of the masters, except in cases of failure after the first year.

The application procedure and eligibility can be found at the official scholarship website: www.unil.ch/international.

CHAPTER 21: FREE E-LEARNING COURSES

If you would prefer to study from the comfort of your home, without the need to travel, there are now a few Universities offering online degrees/courses for free. The first of such University is **University of the People** which is a tuition-free, non-profit, accredited online university dedicated to opening access to higher education globally. University of the People offers online Associates and Bachelor's Degrees in Business Administration and Computer Science.

This was followed by an initiative of MIT and Harvard called EDX which is a learning platform that gives students from any country the opportunity to take free online courses offered by three premier Universities in the US; **Harvard**, **MIT**, and **UC Berkeley**, and about 50+ other Universities and Institutions.

Following this trend, Coursera was introduced which is an online learning platform that partners with the top universities in the world to offer online courses in many fields of study for anyone wishing to take part in for free.

For further information, please go to www.google.com and type in the relevant key words.

COMMONWEALTH
DISTANCE LEARNING

The Commonwealth Distance Learning Scholarships is another of such online scholarships available to candidates from developing commonwealth countries. A full list of developing countries eligible for this scholarship are on their website below. The scholarships cover all tuition fees.

www.cscuk.dfid.gov.uk/apply/distance-learning/info-candidates

EDINBURGH GLOBAL DISTANCE LEARNING

The University of Edinburgh will offer 4 scholarships to citizens of selected developing countries. Each scholarship will cover the full tuition fees over three years.

Email: communications.office@ed.ac.uk

www.ed.ac.uk/student-funding/postgraduate/e-learning/online-masters

Other good general scholarship sources can be gotten from the link below:

www.afterschoolafrica.com/

www.developmentconnection.net

FOR EDUCATION
CONSULTANCY SERVICES

Contact:

CRYSTALINKS EDUCATION

Crystalinks Investment & Services Ltd. (Reg. Number: 09566926)

Info@crystalinkseducation.com

www.crystalinkseducation.com

For within the UK: 0800 999 5649, (Free Phone)

For Outside of the UK: +447460901626 (& WhatsApp)

www.facebook.com/crystalinksis

www.twitter.com/crystalinksis

www.linkedin.com/company/crystalinks-investment-
&-services-ltd

Crystalinks
E D U C A T I O N